Sticky Brains

BY NICOLE LIBIN, Ph.D.

ILLUSTRATED BY CAM MARSOLLIER

Aria was feeling bad.

Really bad.

She didn't feel like

playing
at all

even though her best
friend Zara had come over.

"What's wrong, Aria?" asked Zara.

"This was the worst week ever! Everything was awful!"

"Wow," Zara said. "What happened?"

Aria started to explain, getting madder and **madder** as she talked. She felt like her head was going to burst!

"On Monday
I broke my new laces.

On Tuesday
I fell off my bike

On Wednesday
I made a mess of my
favourite shirt."

"On Thursday, I brought my new race car in for show and tell, but Max had the same car and he showed everyone before I got to.

On Friday, my mom worked late, so I had to stay at school for an extra hour! My whole week was

 bad!"

Zara looked puzzled.

"Wait,
I was with you for most of that."

"You broke your laces on Monday,

but you also got new shoes
with lightning bolts on them.

You fell off your bike on Tuesday

because you were trying to ride with no hands. And you did it!

You dropped ice cream on your shirt on Wednesday,

but your dad said he could clean it.

On Thursday, you and Max were playing together
with your cars all recess. Even the big kids watched.

And I thought your mom worked late Friday so she
could take you camping over the weekend.

See, the week

wasn't
all bad."

"Yeah, I guess.

I have to go in now.

See you later."

Aria was feeling confused!
She went into the house and found her mom.

"Mom, I think there's something wrong with me. I only remember the bad stuff that happens. It makes me feel like I'm bad too."

Her mom gave her a hug. "Oh sweetheart, that sounds very frustrating. And can I tell you a secret?"

"Sure."

"I sometimes feel that way too."

"Really?"

"Yes. So does your dad. Almost everyone feels like that some of the time."

Her mom started to explain.

"A long,
long time ago..."

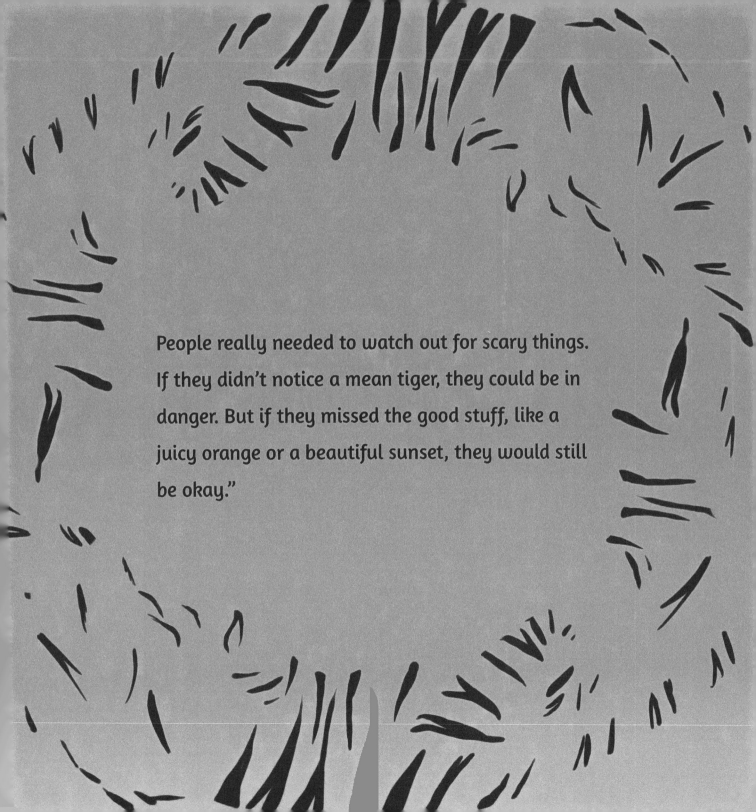

People really needed to watch out for scary things. If they didn't notice a mean tiger, they could be in danger. But if they missed the good stuff, like a juicy orange or a beautiful sunset, they would still be okay."

"So our brains learned to focus on the bad stuff

because that's what helped us stay

safe.

But bad thoughts are like glue,

they stick to us

even if we don't want them to.

This can make us feel like everything is bad

or even that we're bad too."

"So, bad thoughts are stickier than good ones?" asked Aria.

"Yes," replied her mom. "The stuff we think is bad, scary, or sad is really sticky. Our brains see it more and remember it longer. So it's not just you who sees the bad more than the good. Everyone gets stuck sometimes."

"Well I don't want to be stuck!"

yelled Aria.

Her mom smiled. "But there's really good news, too . . .

First, we don't have to get mad at ourselves if we feel sad or if we get stuck on the bad stuff.

And we can do something about it! We can actually change our brains to let go of the bad and see more of the good.

The more we practice, the stronger our brains will be."

"Do you remember when you were just learning to ride your bike?"

Aria nodded. "It was really hard at first. I fell a bunch of times."

"But the more you did it, the easier it got, right?"

Aria nodded again. "Yeah,

I'm aweSome at it now!"

"Our brains work the same way. They get good at what they practice."

"So, we can change our brains to see bad things in a

new way?"

"Yes," her mom replied, "instead of getting stuck, we can choose what we want to notice."

Aria started to think about this.

"If I practice, it would help me to see that things aren't all bad. My brain was showing me only part of the picture."

Her mom smiled again.

"Right!

And we can teach our brains to see more of the good stuff more of the time.

Why don't we try it right now? When something good happens,

let's help the feeling stick."

"First, we can take a few deep breaths.

Now, let's find something that makes us

feel good.

It can be something big like a beautiful rainbow

or getting a birthday present

or even something small like

a cool sip of water."

"Let's pay attention

to how the good things make us feel inside.

Then we can soak in the good feelings."

"WOW!"

said Aria, "It's pretty easy
to change my brain."

"So remember,

even when everything feels awful,

you can train your brain to stick less to the bad and notice more of the good.

You just need to practice it . . .

until it sticks!"

The next week, Aria and Zara were walking to school.

All of a sudden, Aria tripped and fell.

said Zara, "is this another horrible week?"

Aria felt her face getting hot. She started to get mad again.

But then she remembered her **brain-changing powers!**

She took a deep breath and decided to feel the warm sun on her face.

It worked! She felt better!

"Well, I got in trouble for not cleaning my room, I lost my pony sunglasses, and my unicorn shirt ripped," she said.

"But, I also got to play outside, climb trees, and help my dad bake bread!"

Then she smiled and thought to herself:

"I wonder how I will change
my brain next week!"

Using Your Mind to Change Your Brain

Negativity Bias

The idea that Aria and her mom talk about in the book, how bad thoughts are stickier than good ones, is known as the negativity bias. Negativity means the stuff you don't like: stuff you think is bad, gloomy, or unpleasant. Bias means being more likely to think about or notice one thing over another.

Neuroplasticity

The power to change your brain by paying attention is called neuroplasticity. Neuro means brain. Plasticity is like soft clay: you can mold it and change the way it works. By focusing more on the good and letting the bad stuff come and go without blaming yourself, you can train your brain to be less likely to react or get upset and more likely to enjoy what's happening right now. Science shows that you can even change your brain's shape . . . just by paying attention!

Mindfulness

Mindfulness is all about noticing what's happening right now without judging it. You can be mindful of what's going on inside of you (your thoughts, feelings, and your body) and you can be mindful of what's on the outside too (what you hear, see, smell, taste, and touch). Mindfulness lets you be kind and curious about whatever is going on. That means you can choose what you want to do about it and decide what you want to focus on instead of getting caught up in bad thoughts or calling yourself mean names. It's one of the easiest ways to change your brain because all you need is yourself!

How Can I Practice This?

Here are a few more exercises you can do to change your brain:

1. Press Pause

At any time, anyone can take a moment to pause. Wherever you are, take a deep breath and notice how you feel in your body. Can you feel your breath going in and out? Are your fingers tingling? How many toes can you feel without wiggling them? Do you feel heavy or light? Warm or cool? Then take three big breaths. Notice how you feel after you breathe.

You can use this if you start to get upset or frustrated or any time you feel like you need a break. Pausing and really exploring what your body feels like helps you let go of any bad or mean thoughts that might be running through your mind at that moment.

You can even make Pause Buttons! Get a button to keep in your pocket or by your bed, or tie a string through it to make a bracelet you can wear. Use your Pause Button as a reminder that you can stop and take a pause and a breath whenever you need it.

2. Exploring Your Senses

Take a moment to stop and explore what's happening right now, using all of your senses. What colours or shapes can you see? What do you hear far away or up close? What can you smell? How many things can you taste? How does your body feel right now? What can you feel with your fingers or toes? You can even imagine you're an alien from outer space and everything is totally new to you!

You don't need to decide if something is good or bad; see if you can just notice and be curious about it. It's amazing to discover all the different things you can be aware of if you stop to notice. And it helps you choose what you want to pay more attention to more often.

3. The Weather Inside

Use this exercise as a chance to notice how you're feeling and to do your best to be with your feelings just as they are. Ask yourself: what's the weather like inside me right now? It could be dark and stormy, bright and sunny, cloudy, hazy, or maybe freezing and blustery. See if you can be curious and watch it come and go, like you would watch clouds in the sky. Happiness, sadness, anger, and fear happen inside all of us just like snow, rain, and sun happen outside. You might not ask for them or even be able to control them, but if you notice them, you can remember that, just like the weather, they will come and go. And you can be kind and gentle to yourself while they are around.

4. Being Grateful

This simple exercise can be done at any point throughout the day. All you have to do is find something that you are grateful for or something that makes you happy. Just like Aria does in the book, you can focus on something big like your birthday or your last trip to Gramma's house, or something small like a soft blanket. Take a moment to really notice how it makes you feel in your body. See if you can truly enjoy that feeling.

You can also write down or draw your gratitudes and keep them in a special Gratitude Jar that you decorate with your family.

About the Author

Dr. Nicole Libin is a certified mindfulness educator, adjunct professor, and author of Mindful Parenting in a Chaotic World and 5-Minute Mindfulness Meditations for Teens.

She has led mindfulness workshops, classes, and retreats for adults, adolescents, and children, and anyone else who will let her stop and take a breath with them. She has taught and designed mindfulness curricula and other courses for Mindful Schools, Mount Royal University, and private organizations.

As an expert worrier, Nicole decided to write this book when, like Aria, she realized she didn't have to be stuck focusing on the negative. She's still working on it . . .

Nicole lives in Calgary with her husband Cam and her daughter Aria (who really does love unicorns).

About the Illustrator

Cam is many things, but an artist isn't one of them. He tries very hard though. He's ridiculously in love with his wife and daughter who are more amazing than a personalized barn full of unicorns, and twice as inspiring.

FriesenPress

Suite 300 - 990 Fort St
Victoria, BC, V8V 3K2
Canada

www.friesenpress.com

Nicole@followyourbreath.com

Illustrator: Cam Marsollier

ISBN
978-1-5255-5685-2 (Hardcover)
978-1-5255-5686-9 (Paperback)
978-1-5255-5687-6 (eBook)

1. JUVENILE NONFICTION, HEALTH & DAILY LIVING, MINDFULNESS & MEDITATION

Distributed to the trade by The Ingram Book Company

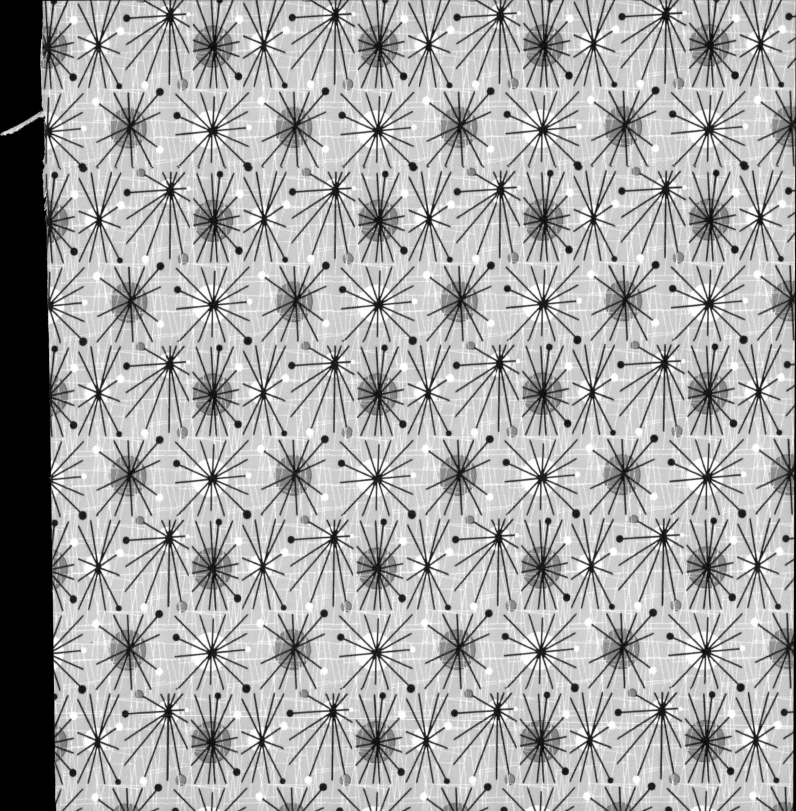

CPSIA information can be obtained
at www.ICGtesting.com
Printed in the USA
BVHW021448170720
583886BV00002B/7

9 781525 556852